GW00597778

# THE LITTLE POTATO BOOK

Susan Fleming

PIATKUS

© 1987 Judy Piatkus (Publishers) Limited

First published in 1987 by
Judy Piatkus (Publishers) Limited,
5 Windmill Street, London W1P 1HF

British Library Cataloguing in Publication Data

The little potato book.
1. Cookery (Potatoes)
I. Fleming, Susan
641.6′521     TX803.P8

ISBN 0-86188-670-4

Drawings by Trevor Newton
Designed by Susan Ryall
Cover photograph by John Lee

Phototypeset in 10 on 11pt Linotron Plantin by
Phoenix Photosetting, Chatham
Printed and bound in Great Britain by
The Bath Press, Avon

# CONTENTS

'Though the potato is an excellent root, deserving to be brought into general use, yet it seems not likely that the use of it should ever be normal in the country.'

David Davies, *The Case of the Labourers in Husbandry*, 1795

# THE POTATO

The potato is such a familiar and everyday vegetable that most of us tend to ignore it, buying
colourful newcomers with enthusiasm, but stocking
up with just any old spud. Potatoes may be the most
bought and consumed vegetable in the western
world – the dependable and comforting basic filler –
but in fact they are much more interesting than this,
with their recent and extraordinary history, their
culinary versatility, and their high nutritional value.

Potatoes, popularly thought of as a root vegetable,
are in fact tubers, swollen underground stems that
serve the plant as storage organs. The plant itself
grows from 2–3 feet (60–90cm) high, with white or
purple flowers, and seed-bearing fruit rather like
small tomatoes. It is the tubers, rather than the
actual seed, which are more normally used for pro-
pagating new plants. The 'eyes' of potatoes are actually buds, each of which can form a new plant in the
following year.

The potato – or *solanum tuberosum* – belongs to the
*Solanaceae* family, which includes more than 2,000
species found mainly in tropical America. The

1

family is of considerable economic importance as it not only includes food plants such as potato, tomato, aubergine, sweet and hot red peppers, but also tobacco, and a number of highly poisonous plants such as deadly nightshade and henbane, used in drug manufacture.

Potatoes, sadly, are not immune to family characteristics, and they too contain a poisonous alkaloid, called solanine. This is present in all green parts of the plant – the stems, leaves and fruit – and none of these should ever be eaten. Likewise, the seeds of potatoes, and of tomatoes, should never be sprouted like mung beans or alfalfa seeds. Green developing on tubers exposed to light – they are producing chlorophyll – should be deeply peeled off, or the tuber discarded. The slight traces of solanine present in the tubers are thought to contribute to the potato's characteristic flavour and are rendered harmless by cooking.

# WHAT'S IN A NAME?

The sweet potato (*ipomoea batatas*) was the first to be introduced to Europe, and the first to be called potato (from the Spanish *patata*, deriving from the Arawak *batata*). Gradually, the other tuber, *solanum tuberosum*, acquired the exclusive use of the name, the former being distinguished by the word 'sweet'. *Solanum* comes from the Latin for comforting, and refers to the sedative properties of many of the Solanaceae family.

'Pratie' is a common name for the potato throughout Ireland, and 'taters' is universally used in Wales and England. The 'tatties' of Scotland is an example of the Scots' love of the affectionate diminutive, 'ie', and schoolchildren there have 'tattie-howking' (potato-lifting) holidays at harvest time. 'Spud' is another familiar name for the potato, particularly in Scotland, and comes from the name for a three-pronged fork used to lift potatoes. (A 'spuddy' is a man who sells bad potatoes.)

'Murphy' is a name common in Ireland, and used in America too – and must have referred to some particularly successful potato grower. Hence the Spike-Murphy, a medieval-looking implement upon which potatoes to be baked are impaled, the metal spikes conducting heat through the flesh.

# A GLOBAL HISTORY OF THE POTATO

The brave Walter Raleigh,
Queen Bess's own knight,
Brought here from Virginia
The root of delight.
By him it was planted
At Youghal so gay;
An' sure Munster praties
Are famed to this day.

*Popular Songs of Ireland*,
Crofton Croker, 1886

The potato is native to South America, and was discovered by the conquering Spanish in Peru in about 1536. A member of one expedition wrote of plants with 'floury roots' which were 'of good flavour, a gift very acceptable to the Indians, and a dainty dish even for Spaniards.'

For the Incas, potatoes were a staple, whether eaten fresh, dried as flour, or fermented into a beer. They had even invented a freeze-drying process by which the tubers could be preserved – as *chuno* – for times of crop failure or hardship. Potatoes featured considerably in their culture, and many of their pots were made in the shape of potatoes, eyes and all.

Potatoes had been introduced to Spain by 1569 or earlier, but there is no reliable evidence for the arrival of the potato in Britain before the 1580s. Sir Francis Drake is thought by many to have been responsible, and because of this Germany, now one of the world's great potato-eating countries, erected a statue of him holding a potato flower (removed by the Nazis in the 1940s). However, Sir Walter Raleigh is more popularly believed to have introduced both tobacco and the potato, and it was certainly at his Irish estate, Youghal, that the potato was first cultivated in about 1590. Some people believed that the potato colonised western Ireland after tubers floated ashore from the wrecked Armada.

The first recorded mention of the potato – and an illustration – was in John Gerard's herbal of 1597, where he described it as being 'of Virginia'. It had probably been taken *to* Virginia from South America as ships' stores, and thence to England, hence his mistake. This annotation remained in use for some time, primarily to distinguish it from *batatas* or the sweet potato, an earlier introduction. It was not until about 1710 that the potato became known as the 'common', 'English' or, more significantly, the 'Irish' potato.

# THE POTATO IN IRELAND

By 1650, the potato had become the staple food of Ireland, and this fact was to influence the history not only of Ireland but also of England and America. As Ireland's climate was too wet for major grain cultivation, and the people were increasingly being driven to the areas least favourable for grain crop cultivation (by English landlords on the whole), only the potato could be grown as food. It could survive in poorer soils, it needed little cultivation, it could be harvested by hand, and it didn't need to be threshed, ground or baked. As comparatively little work was involved, and small plots could support whole families, the potato is said to be the means whereby Ireland became *over*-populated, with at least 9 million people by 1840. (If the Irish had been grain or bread fed, the whole land area would only have enabled 5 million to survive.) As it was, most of Ireland seemed to be permanently on the verge of starvation anyway. More than a century earlier, Jonathan Swift's *Modest Proposal*, whereby Irish babies could be fattened to feed the starving populace, was his satirical response to the horrific conditions that existed in his country.

But when the potato blight hit the whole of Europe in 1845–6, it was Ireland, a one-crop country, that was the most tragically devastated. It has been estimated that up to a million Irish died of starvation and consequent diseases. This was followed by the emigration of at least 1½ million, an exodus that reached its peak at the time of the First World War, and still continues today.

Many illiterate Irish peasants went to England where they were sourly received, although Carlyle was to credit the rapid growth of British manufacturing industry to the labour of cheap potato-fed Irishmen. Even more Irish went to North America, and thus it could with justification be argued that there would have been no Kennedy as president of the United States if it had not been for the potato.

## THE POTATO IN EUROPE

The potato was viewed with great suspicion all over Europe, a suspicion that lasted for centuries. Its appearance was unpleasant – rather warty and scabby – and so it was thought to be a probable cause of leprosy, the dread skin disease of the time. Another, marginally more scientific, explanation for its slow start might be that these early potatoes contained more solanine than they do now, and eating them could have caused rashes, an early symptom of leprosy.

The principal reason, however, for this early distaste – apart from the potato's recognised familial relationship with deadly nightshade – was that the potato was the first plant ever in Europe to be grown from tubers and not from seed. And as the cultivation and behaviour of the plant were so completely unfamiliar, it is not surprising that eating its 'fruit' was not over-popular initially.

The Burgundians were actually forbidden to make use of the tubers because of the fear of leprosy. Scrofula in Switzerland, and consumption, rickets and fever elsewhere, were also attributed to potato eating. At the very least, potatoes were believed to be extremely flatulent, aphrodisiac – to 'excite Venus' – and to be fit only for slaves or swine.

The Puritans and Presbyterian Scots were violently against the new vegetable as it was ungodly, not having been mentioned in the Bible!

From being a luxury food of the rich in 17th century, in the 18th, for economic reasons, the potato was encouraged to become the staple food of the poor throughout Europe. This met with considerable resistance. In Prussia, Frederick the Great had to 'persuade' his starving people to eat potatoes by force; and their inclusion in workhouse soups in Munich had to be kept strictly secret. Today, Germany is one of the major potato producing and consuming countries.

In France, Louis XVI was interested in foods that might save his people from the recurring famines of the 1760s and 1770s, and it was one Monsieur Parmentier who suggested the potato as a solution. He had first encountered it during the Seven Years' War when a prisoner of war in Prussia. Later he grew potatoes in a field outside Paris, arousing the cupidity of the Parisians by ostentatiously guarding the field during the day, and as ostentatiously neglecting to do so at night! He gave a dinner at which all the courses, including the sweet, were made from potatoes, and even persuaded Marie Antoinette to wear potato flowers in her hair. Many classic French

potato dishes are named after Parmentier, and France now uses the potato more than any other vegetable.

In Britain the fact that potatoes were the major food of the immigrant Irish, for whom the English had little but contempt, didn't help. But, as on the

Continent, war and subsequent grain shortages led to its gradual adoption. The high cost of flour was a great incentive, with potatoes often being baked into bread to supplement the flour. By the end of the 18th century, the potato was the most important vegetable crop in Britain, and it was probably then that the British reliance on potatoes as an integral part of a meal ('meat and two veg') originated.

The complete rehabilitation of the potato in Britain came about during the two wars of the 20th century: in a 1944 Stationery Office publication, it was claimed that 'In 1917, it was only because we had a very good stock of potatoes in hand, that we survived the critical U-Boat period.' And Lord Woolton, Minister of Food in the 1939–45 war, waxed enthusiastic about the potato in his 'Potato Plan': potatoes had to 'go into action on the Food Front', and people were told to grow potatoes instead of relying on imported grain: 'You can save shipping by eating potatoes instead of bread. The potatoes are here; they are a healthy food. Let your patriotism direct your appetite: eat potatoes – and if you are a cook, learn new ways of serving them.'

Never healthier than during that wartime period of rationing, the British are still learning about potatoes, and now eat an amazing 230 lb (103kg) per person per year with, in 1985, over 160,000 hectares in England, Scotland, Wales and Northern Ireland planted with potatoes. However, it is still in Russia, Poland and West Germany that the potato is grown and consumed the most – the Russian figure for 1979, some 262 lb (119kg) per capita per year. In

Holland, about 25% of land available is given over to potato cultivation for home consumption and export. In 1982, the Dutch even exported some 5,000 tonnes to the ancestral home of the potato, Peru!

Cyprus is a major grower and exporter, with its own Potato Marketing Board, and Italy, France, Greece, Spain (including the Balearics and Canaries) and Israel all have thriving potato industries. Jersey new potatoes are one of the delights of the potato year – and even some North African countries are now growing potatoes commercially.

It took 150 years for the potato to travel back to the American continent via Ireland – it was first grown as a food crop in 1719 near Londonderry (inevitably), New Hampshire – and now huge acreages are given over to the crop. The potato is the world's best known and most popular vegetable, virtually equalling the wheat crop in volume and value. It is here to stay!

# WHAT THEY SAID
# ABOUT IT

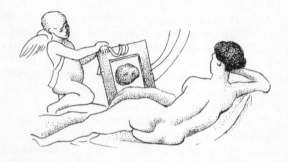

'Nevertheless they are flatulent, and therefore some use them for exciting Venus.'

Clusius, 1601

'Our own people [of the city of Basle] sometimes roast them under embers in the manner of Tubers [truffles], and having taken off the cuticle eat them with pepper; others having roasted them and cleaned them, cut them up into slices and pour on fat sauce with pepper and eat them for exciting Venus, increasing semen; others regard them as useful for invalids since they believe them to be good nourishment. They nourish no less than chestnuts and carrots and are flatulent.'

Swiss botanist, Gaspar Bauhin, 1619

'This root, no matter how you prepare it, is tasteless and floury. It cannot pass for an agreeable food; but it supplies a food sufficiently abundant and sufficiently healthy for men who ask only to sustain themselves . . . The potato is blamed and with reason, for its windiness; but what is a question of wind to the virile organs of the peasant and the workers? . . . an Egyptian fruit whose cultivation may possibly have some value in the colonies.'

Diderot, *L'Encyclopédie*, 1746 ff.

'Potatoes are good for none but swine, and those they won't fatten.'

Sir Archibald Grant, 1757

'The scrofulous are common in Switzerland, where the people support themselves above all on potatoes.'
Daniel Langhouse, *L'Art de Guérir Soi-Même*, 1768

When Mrs Austen, about the year 1770, advised a tenant's wife at Steventon (near Basingstoke) to plant potatoes in her garden, the response was: 'No, no, they are all very well for you gentry, but they must be terribly costly to rear.'

'It is favourable to population; for it has been observed that in the western parts of Ireland where it is almost the only diet of the labouring poor, it is no unusual thing to see six, seven, eight, ten and sometimes more children, the issue of one couple, starting almost naked out of a miserable cabin, upon the approach of an accidental traveller.'

*The Practical Farmer*
*or The Complete English Traveller*,
David Henry, 1771

'The pasty taste, the natural insipidity, the unhealthy quality of this food, which is flatulent and indigestible, has caused it to be rejected from refined households and returned to the people, whose coarse palates and stronger stomachs are satisfied with anything capable of appeasing hunger.'

Legrand d'Aussy,
*Histoire de la Vie Privée des Français*, 1783

# POTATOES VARIOUS

Potatoes come in a multitude of sizes, shapes, colours, textures and varieties. They can be huge (like the 'perfect baker', the Idaho, which grows successfully in America only, in a soil rich in volcanic ash), or tiny, like the new potatoes from Jersey or Egypt; they can be round, kidney-shaped, oval or an odd root ginger shape (the Pink Fir Apple). The potatoes most popular in the UK are those with white or red skins ('Whites' or 'Reds' as they are unimaginatively – and very uninformatively – labelled in greengrocers), but some rarer varieties can be pink, dark blue, purple or black! The flesh, too, varies from creamy white, through lemon and yellow (more popular on the Continent) to (once again rare) a blue-purple.

Next to flavour – which can vary from area to area, from season to season, according to soil and growing conditions – it is the texture of a potato which most concerns the potato buyer. The difference between floury and waxy potatoes is fundamental to the cook if he or she doesn't want a potato to disintegrate when boiled for a salad, or a mash to become slimy when made inadvertently with a waxy potato. (A simple test, according to Harold McGee, is to put potatoes in a brine made of one part salt to eleven parts water: waxy will float, floury will sink.)

First and second early – or new – potatoes (usually available in late May, and in June, July, August and September each year) are waxy in texture. Maincrop potatoes (available from September) are often waxy when 'new' in the autumn, but many become floury after winter storage. Floury potatoes have more starch in their surface layers, which swells when heated and bursts the skin – thus the surface soft mealiness of some potatoes when boiled.

Over 100 different varieties are known in the UK alone, but less than half of those are grown commercially, and perhaps only about 15 are regularly available to the potato buyer. As with so many foodstuffs, the demands of commerce have narrowed the choice down to the potatoes which crop best, resist disease best and store best, or which make the best crisps or will fit into cans most successfully. As a result the best flavours are often bred *out*, and it is up to the home growers, the gardeners, to keep alive the more exotic and historic types – helped along by such expert enthusiasts as Donald MacLean of Dornock Farm, Crieff, who has the biggest private collection of potatoes in the world, some 300 or more varieties.

# GROWING POTATOES
# AT HOME

Potatoes grown at home, particularly new potatoes, have an unbeatable flavour, but they take up a large amount of space. Small plots, however, can produce a crop adequate for most people's needs, and when space is really at a premium, first early or new potatoes can be grown in pots.

## PREPARING THE SOIL

Choose an open site – but not a frost pocket – with plenty of light. Most soils are suitable, although potatoes prefer it deep, fertile and well drained; but even heavy or clay soils can be used, as long as they are prepared well in advance.

In autumn, dig in plenty of well rotted manure or compost. Leave the ground rough so that the winter frosts will break it up further. Just before planting, fork the soil and top dress it with a general fertiliser, raking it in well.

## BUYING AND PREPARING SEED POTATOES

'Seed' potatoes can be ordered or obtained from growers and garden centres from January. It *is* possible to sprout from tubers of home-grown crops, but as these are more vulnerable to disease, it's best to buy certified seed potatoes (virus-free 'seeds' produced in disease-free areas). It's also best to seek advice before choosing the variety, as individual varieties and their success rates vary greatly from area to area.

About 5 lb (2.25kg) seed potatoes will be enough for three 10 feet (3 metre) rows and should give a yield of about 45–65 lb (20–30kg). Choose small seed tubers, from 1–2 oz (25–50g) in weight, about the size of a small hen's egg. Set them out in trays or in fibre eggboxes, with the plump or 'rose' end – the one with the eyes – upwards. Keep in a dry, light, frost-free place, not in sunlight or heat, for 4–5 weeks until the eyes have sturdy sprouts of about ¼–½ inch (6–12 mm) long. The aim of this sprouting – best for first and second earlies – is to allow a few extra weeks of growing without the dangers of frost. This 'chitting' is not so necessary for maincrop varieties as they already have a longer growing season.

# PLANTING POTATOES

Dig drills or little trenches about 4–6 in (10–15cm) deep. If planting first earlies, have drills 24 in (60cm) apart; for second earlies and maincrop, 27–30 in (68–75cm) apart.

Place first earlies in the drills, 12 in (30cm) between tubers, in mid to late March (depending on location and weather). Second earlies and maincrop have 16in (40cm) between tubers. The former are planted in early April, the latter in late April. The sprouts should be uppermost. You could first cover the potatoes with a handful of peat to protect sprouts before raking earth from drills back over the top. Rake up from between rows to make slight ridges over potatoes. Scatter with a little general fertiliser.

When plants are 6–8 in (15–20cm) high, begin earthing up. This increases the depth of soil over the roots, encouraging them to spread and form tubers. Hoe between drills and take up earth around the shoots. Do this every two or three weeks until the ridge is about 6 in (15cm) tall, or until the haulm or potato foliage meets between the rows. Keep all potatoes well watered in dry weather, flooding the trenches between the ridges. Fertilise occasionally too.

Spray second earlies and maincrop potatoes in early July with Bordeaux mixture (or similar) on both top and underside of leaves to prevent blight. Repeat every two weeks until September.

| PEST OR DISEASE | SYMPTOMS AND DAMAGE |
|---|---|
| Potato cyst eelworm | Minute yellow or brown cysts on roots which contain hundreds of eggs (can remain dormant in soil for years). Worms eat into roots causing yellowing, wilting and death. |
| Wireworm | Larvae of click beetles. Tough-skinned, yellow-brown worms among roots bore into tubers. |
| Blackleg | A black rot develops at base of plant, leaves yellow, stems soften and die, and any tubers contain slimy rot. |
| Blight (*phytophthora infestans*) | Leaves develop yellow-brown patches and shrivel in dry weather; in wet conditions, white fungal threads on undersides of leaves. Haulms collapse and tubers rot. |
| Common scab | Raised scabs on tuber skin, but flesh not affected. |
| Powdery scab | Raised scabs that later burst in brown powdery mass. |
| Wart disease | Large warty growths on tuber skin which causes tubers to disintegrate. Must be reported to Ministry of Agriculture. |

| DANGER PERIOD | PREVENTION AND TREATMENT |
|---|---|
| July–Sept | A fertile soil is vital. Rotate crops regularly, and if infestation is severe, do not plant potatoes again for at least 5 years. Grow resistant varieties. |
| March–Sept | Common on newly cultivated land. Apply BAC, bromophos or diazinon to soil around plants to disinfect. |
| June | Buy only certified seed and destroy all affected plants. |
| May–August | In wet season, when risk is greatest, spray at 10–14 day intervals with maneb, zineb or Bordeaux mixture, starting just before foliage stretches across rows. Grow resistant varieties, and rotate crops. Destroy all affected plants. |
| growing season | Grow resistant varieties. Do not lime soil; manure and water well. |
| growing season | Grow resistant varieties. Dig up and destroy affected plants, and do not plant on same site for a few years. |
| growing season | Buy only certified seed of resistant varieties. Destroy all affected plants. |

# POTATO PESTS AND DISEASES

As well as the pests and diseases on the chart, potatoes also come under attack from slugs, snails and aphids. The Colorado beetle, although rare in the UK, has been known to appear (it invaded the Jersey potato fields, for instance, during the German occupation). Its presence must be reported to the Ministry of Agriculture: do so by informing the police who usually have its 'mug shot' on display. (Interestingly, Germany accused Britain in 1939 of airlifting the beetles on to her potato fields in an attempt to subvert the Reich! And in 1950, the USSR accused the US of the same crime in East Germany.)

To safeguard your potato crop in general, use certified seed, employ good soil hygiene, and rotate crops as much as possible. If using chemicals, do so carefully, always following the manufacturer's instructions – but use organic preparations if at all possible.

# HARVESTING POTATOES

Early potatoes should be ready in about three months from planting, in June to July, when the flowers are fully open. Tubers about the size of hen's eggs are ready; smaller ones should be left to continue growing. New potatoes should really be harvested straight from the ground to the pot. If you want to store them for a couple of days (no more), let them dry a little first.

Second earlies can be harvested from July to early September, and can be stored if necessary. Maincrop varieties – and those wanted for winter storage – will not be ready until September or early October when the foliage has died down.

Choose a dry day for lifting potato crops. Cut off and discard (burn) the haulm or foliage to make lifting easier. Insert a garden fork well clear of the plant so that it can be lifted in one go. Take care not to bruise or damage any potatoes as these will not store. Pick up *all* the tubers, however small, as any missed could be the cause of disease or pests in the future. Leave the potatoes to dry for a couple of hours before storing.

# Storing Home-Grown Potatoes

Only maincrop potatoes should be stored. Choose healthy, undamaged tubers (use damaged ones immediately or discard), and make sure they are thoroughly dry (the skin should not come off when rubbed with your thumb).

Potatoes can be stored in an earth 'clamp' in the garden but, more practical for the average grower-cook, they are best in a cool, dry, frost-free and dark outhouse, shed or cellar. Keep them away from strong-smelling substances such as petrol or paint. Place in boxes with raised corner posts which stack to allow air circulation and easy inspection. Paper or hessian sacks are often used, but one hidden rotten potato can infect dozens of others. *Never* use plastic sacks as this cuts out air. Potatoes can also be stored on a dry floor covered with straw.

Inspect stored potatoes regularly and, from January, rub off sprouts.

# POT-GROWN POTATOES

For a special luxurious treat, town dwellers can grow a few first earlies in pots in January or February.

Line the bottom of a 12 in (30cm) pot with crocks, and cover with about 2 in (5cm) of John Innes No. 3 compost. Dampen, then place one or two seed potatoes in the compost, sprouts or eyes uppermost. Cover with more compost to a depth of about 1 in (2.5cm). As shoots grow, add more compost at intervals. Water and fertilise regularly. After about 12–14 weeks, potatoes can be harvested.

Proverb:   Plant your taters when you will
             They won't come up before April.

# BUYING POTATOES

**B**uy only firm, bright looking potatoes, and those that have not been greened by exposure to light. It's better to pay a little more for potatoes which are loose and still dirty than to buy washed potatoes (the high-pressure hoses can damage the skin) or those sealed in polythene which makes them sweat – *and* lets the light in. The advent of washed potatoes packed in peat in paper sacks, however, can confuse even the most watchful buyer.

Potatoes should be smooth, free of disease, with no sprouts and few eyes. The British Potato Marketing Board lays down very strict rulings, and grades them for size. Maincrop potatoes should be dry and the skin should not be able to be rubbed off. The reverse is true for new: they should feel slightly damp, and the skin should rub off easily.

Buy and use new potatoes as you need them. Store small quantities of maincrop in a dark, cool, easily accessible place. If buying in quantity from farmers, in sacks perhaps, store as home-grown (see above).

'Potatoes, three pounds a penny, Potatoes,
Augh fait, there's a kind-hearted lass of green Erin,
Unruffled in mind and for trifles not caring
Who, trundling her barrow, content in her state is
Still crying, three pounds for a penny Potatoes.'
*Cries of London*, Samuel Syntax, 1820

# THE FOOD VALUE OF POTATOES

The potato has had a bad press since it arrived in Europe: first it was thought to cause leprosy, now it is said to be fattening. In fact, it is very nutritious and useful in the daily diet.

Chemically, a potato's composition is as follows: water 81%; starch 16%; minerals and trace elements 1%; vitamins 0.7%; fibre 0.6%; protein 0.35%; sugar 0.27%; and fat 0.08%.

Because of that high water content, and despite the starch or carbohydrate content, potatoes are not the stodge so frequently condemned. They are only a modest source of energy, containing about 22 calories per 1 oz (25g) when plain boiled – and this represents, in the average British daily intake of about 6 oz (175g) potatoes, just a twentieth of the daily energy needs. It is the oil in which potatoes are cooked, or the butter put on top, that makes them fattening!

Interestingly, a recent investigation into single-food diets involved 23 Irishmen who volunteered to eat ten large jacket-baked potatoes a day for three months. Most lost weight, although they were allowed other foods *after* eating the potatoes! It's probable none had any room left, but the weight loss was predictable because even that enormous quantity of potatoes represents fewer calories than the average male body needs daily (about 1,250 as opposed to up to 2,900).

The mineral and vitamin contents would seem to be negligible, but, still working on that daily 6 oz (175g), potatoes provide approximately 4% of our total intake of protein (the quality of which is said to be as high as that of eggs); 8% of our intake of iron, and the following approximate percentages of our intake of vitamins: 10% thiamin, 3% riboflavin; 9% nicotinic acid and 24% vitamin C. The recommended daily intake of the latter vitamin, for instance, is 30 mg in the UK (60 mg in the USA), and the C content of a medium potato baked in its jacket (about 4–5 oz/125g) is a massive 10.4 mg. Potatoes are thus a most important source of Vitamin C, and care must always be taken to preserve it. Vitamin C can be lost through storage (C decreases the longer a vegetable is out of the ground), by peeling (most of the nutrients are in or near the skin), and by cooking (C and some other nutrients are water soluble). Mashing and keeping potatoes warm also slightly lessens the C content.

Another significant nutrient is potassium, and potatoes are one of the richest food sources. Potassium counters the effects of sodium or salt, of which there is excess in western diets and which contributes to high blood pressure and heart disease. Thus potatoes, especially those organically grown, can actually be viewed in this respect as a food which *promotes* health.

If potatoes baked or boiled in their skins are the richest source of Vitamin C, so they are also rich in dietary fibre. The recommended British daily intake is 30g; a baked potato eaten with its skin contains 5g, once again a significant proportion. The best-selling *F-Plan Diet* has a whole chapter of baked potato recipes.

The principal dietary drawback concerning potatoes is their solanine content, and very green tubers should be discarded (sprouts should not even be fed to livestock). In the early 70s, eating blight-affected potatoes in pregnancy was linked by some researchers to infants born with anencephaly and spina bifida. This view was subsequently shown to be invalid and was withdrawn.

# POTATO PRODUCTS

According to the Potato Marketing Board flow chart in Great Britain for June 1984–May 1985, 24% of the total home crop of potatoes for human consumption (over 1¼ million tonnes) went to the processing industry. Some potatoes were imported for processing purposes, and of the resultant total of 1,676,000 tonnes, 47% was frozen, 36.2% made into crisps, 14.2% dried and 2.5% canned.

We obviously eat a lot of frozen chips and other potato snack foods, and although these will contain a good proportion of potato nutrients, all are more calorie high because of the oil in which they are fried. The sodium or salt content has caused concern too, but a recent nutritional survey into crisps – on which the British spend £650 million a year, eating a staggering 100 million packets per week – has shown that the average bag contains less salt than a slice of white bread or bowl of breakfast cereal, as well as ten times the energy and six times the vitamin C of an apple.

Potato crisps were invented in Saratoga Springs, New York State, in 1853 by a Red Indian chef who was asked to produce a thinner chip – and crisps are still called chips by the Americans.

Dehydrated or dried potatoes have a long history. The Incas started it with *chuno* and, since the late 18th century, experiments have been made to provide potatoes in a form more portable and durable as ships' stores, as combatants' rations in wartime and,

nowadays, as something which lasts, packs more easily and densely, and which can be prepared quickly in the home – instant mash. Vitamins and other nutrients are now *added* to instant mashes (without, they contain two-thirds the Vitamin C of fresh), and despite the little tin aliens of the award-winning TV commercial (who became hysterical at the thought of someone actually bothering to *peel* a potato), fresh potatoes are still nutritionally best.

Potato flour, too, has a long history and some positive benefits. It is of special importance to those on gluten-free diets, and is vital in some cake and biscuit recipes, giving a softer texture. Canned potatoes have much the same nutritive value as freshly cooked tubers, with slightly less Vitamin C.

# POTATO STARCH

Starch was a necessity of fashionable life from the 16th century onwards, and the Elizabethans used the roots of the wild arum (other names are Lords and Ladies, Cuckoo Pint or Starchwort) to stiffen the fine lace used on their cuffs and ruffs. Starch was also needed by dyers, printers, hairpowder and wig makers, and many basic ingredients were researched for their stiffening properties. Cereals, rice cooking water, and the potato were tried. The potato proved particularly good for sizing paper and textiles, and for adding the finish to fine cotton goods.

'To make potato starch: Peel and grate several large raw potatoes into a basin of cold water and stir well. Let them steep, squeezing the pulp in your hands, then pour off the water and let it stand till the starch can be seen settled at the bottom. Pour off the water and dry out the starch.' (*Water in England*, Dorothy Hartley, Macdonald & Jane's, 1978)

# POTATO ALCOHOL

Alcohol can be distilled from virtually anything fermentable, and in this potatoes have played a not undistinguished part. The natives of ancient Peru brewed a beer from them and, following the gradual spread of the potato throughout Europe, Russia, Poland and Germany used them in the making of vodka and schnapps. The Scandinavians also used potatoes as the base for aquavit. But the potato spirit which is most famous (or infamous) is the poteen of Ireland, the product of the illicit stills.

Potatoes also make a wine, when mixed with raisins, demerara sugar, wheat, boiling water and yeast. If kept for some years, it resembles brandy, according to Dorothy Hartley in *Food in England* (Macdonald, 1954).

'Excellent,' he [James Bond] said to the barman, 'but if you can get a vodka made with grain instead of potatoes, you will find it still better.'
*Casino Royale*, Ian Fleming, Jonathan Cape, 1953.

'A diet that consists predominantly of rice leads to the use of opium, just as a diet which consists predominantly of potatoes leads to the use of liquor.'
Nietzsche, c. 1880.

Murphy has invented a new method of fishing. He only has to sprinkle a pint or two of poteen into the river and the salmon come up ready canned.
Irish joke

# COOKING POTATOES

Always choose the right type of potato for the cooking method. Don't refrigerate, as they become sweet. Peel only if absolutely necessary, because of the nutrients under the skin; use a proper potato peeler or, better still, boil in their skins and then peel (you lose less potato). Peeled potatoes turn brown through oxygenation, so either cook immediately or keep for a few hours in clear water. If you have potatoes that tend to turn brown *after* cooking (due to the iron content), add a little lemon juice to the water. Keep potato cooking water for soup or gravy, as a certain amount of the vegetable's nutrients will have leached out.

BOILED    Scrub old potatoes well, cutting out eyes. Cut into even sizes if necessary. Put in enough cold salted water just to cover and boil gently until tender. Boil new potatoes as on page 51.

STEAMED    Cooking in a steamer or pressure cooker means fewer nutrients are lost. Scrub well and steam *over* salted boiling water until tender.

MASHED    Mash with butter, cream and seasonings (see page 50). Mashed potatoes can be bound with egg yolks, flavoured with cheese or herbs, and made into **croquettes**; roll in flour and breadcrumbs, then deep-fry. **Duchesse** potatoes are made from a simple 1 lb (450g) mash, using 2 oz (50g) butter, seasonings and 2 egg yolks: pipe in twirl shapes on a buttered baking sheet and brown in a hot oven, or use as a piped border for other foods. **Dauphine** potatoes consist of the duchesse mixture mixed with a choux paste which is then piped or spooned into fat and deep-fried.

SHALLOW-FRIED/SAUTÉED Waxy old potatoes are best for this. Use a good vegetable oil or, for the best flavour, olive oil, duck or goose fat. Par-boil peeled potatoes and then slice. Fry fairly slowly in the hot fat until brown on both sides and drain well. (If you add fried onions, the dish becomes *pommes de terre Lyonnaise*.)

DEEP-FRIED Cut peeled potatoes into various shapes, rinse in cold water, then dry thoroughly. Fry larger shapes, in batches, in a good vegetable oil at an initial temperature of 360°F/185°C without browning. Drain, then fry again at 390°F/195°C to brown.

Cut into chips about ½ in (1.25cm) thick; cut into smaller chips (the national obsession of Belgium, *frites*) or matchsticks; cut into crisps or game chips; or cut on the corrugated blade of a mandoline for waffles or *gaufrette* potatoes. Make potato 'baskets' from *gaufrettes*: overlap in a potato nest maker then deep-fry in the mould.

ROASTED Potatoes can be roasted from raw, but about 6–8 minutes' prior par-boiling makes for a crisper crust and fluffier inside. Use dripping, or cook around roast meat. At 375°F/190°C/Gas 5 they will take about 45–60 minutes.

BAKED  Many enthusiasts swear by a mixture of salt and oil rubbed over the potato skin first to make it crispy; restaurateur John Tovey bakes his potatoes embedded in a tray of coarse salt; and others claim the best baked potato is that wrapped in foil and cooked in the embers of a bonfire. Use large, smooth, floury potatoes, and *bash* them open (in a teatowel) rather than cut, as this makes them softer.

POTATO PASTRY  This has been around at least since the war years, when potatoes were used to eke out rationed flour. Use potato pastry for any of your favourite recipes. To make 4 oz (125g) pastry, use 4 oz (125g) plain flour, 2 oz (50g) cooked and sieved potatoes, 2 oz (50g) fat (half butter or margarine, half lard) and a pinch of salt.

'Here's taters hot, my little chaps,
Now just lay out a copper,
I'm known up and down the Strand
You'll not find any hotter.'

Baked potato seller
(potatoes often used for warming
hands in muffs!) in *London Cries*, 1813

# SOME GOOD COOKING VARIETIES

**Boiled**
*Earlies:* Arran Comet, Estima, Home Guard, Maris Peer, Pentland Javelin, Ulster Sceptre, Wilja.
*Maincrop:* Cara, Desirée, King Edward, Maris Piper, Pentland Ivory, Redskin, Romano.

**Mashed**
Desirée, Golden Wonder, Kerrs Pink, King Edward, Maris Piper, Pentland Hawk, Redskin.

**Jacket-baked**
Arran Comrade, Cara, Desirée, Epicure, Golden Wonder, King Edward, Maris Piper, Pentland Crown, Pentland Dell, Pentland Hawk, Pentland Ivory, Pentland Squire, Romano.

**Deep-fried**
*Earlies:* Arran Comet, Maris Peer, Red Craig's Royal, Ulster Sceptre.
*Maincrop:* Desirée, Golden Wonder, King Edward, Majestic, Maris Piper, Pentland Dell.

**Roast**
*Earlies:* Maris Peer.
*Maincrop:* Cara, Desirée, Golden Wonder, King Edward, Majestic, Maris Piper, Pentland Dell.

**Salad**
Most earlies, particularly Arran Comet, Arran Pilot, Duke of York, Craig's Royal, as well as Pink Fir Apple, Desirée, Golden Wonder and Wilja.

# POTATO RECIPES

## POTAGE PARMENTIER

A variation of one of the recipes named after the saviour of the potato in France. Serve it hot with some croûtons; serve it chilled with a swirl of cream – when it becomes Vichyssoise.

*4 large leeks, white part only, trimmed*
*2 oz (50g) butter*
*4 medium potatoes, peeled and diced*
*salt and freshly ground black pepper*
*1½ pints (900ml) chicken stock*
*½ pint (300ml) milk*
*snipped chives*
*2 tablespoons cream*

Cut the leeks in half lengthways and slice thinly. Soak in cold water to clean, then drain well.

Melt the butter in a large pan, and add the leeks, potatoes and seasoning to taste. Stir, then sweat over a low heat for about 15–20 minutes.

Add the stock and milk, bring to a simmer, then cover and simmer for a further 20 minutes. Purée in a liquidizer, then pour through a sieve into the cleaned saucepan. Reheat gently, stirring in the snipped chives and cream just before serving.

Serves 4

# BAKED SOUFFLÉ POTATOES

The potatoes may be baked simply until tender as below, then opened and garnished with a variety of fillings. Try salted butter, crispy diced bacon, grated Cheddar, soured cream and chives, *pesto*, mashed avocado or lumpfish roe.

*4 medium potatoes, washed*
*1 oz (25g) butter*
*salt and freshly ground black pepper*
*4 oz (125g) Cheddar cheese, grated*
*2 teaspoons grainy mustard*
*2 eggs, separated*

Preheat the oven to 375°F/190°C/Gas 5, and bake the potatoes on a baking sheet for about 1¼–1½ hours or until tender.

Cut a lengthways slice off the top of each potato, and scoop out soft flesh into a bowl. Be careful not to pierce the skin shell. Mash the potato flesh smooth, then mix in the butter, seasonings to taste, Cheddar cheese, mustard and egg yolks. Mix together thoroughly.

Whip the egg whites until stiff but not dry, then fold into the potato mixture. Pile back into the skin shells, and return to the oven for a further 15–20 minutes or until well risen and golden.

Serves 4

# POTATO SKINS WITH SOURED CREAM DIP

A fairly recent and delicious idea which originated in America and is good as a starter. Use the scooped-out insides in any other dish requiring mashed potato.

*5 large potatoes, scrubbed*
*vegetable oil, for deep-frying*
*¼ pint (150ml) soured cream*
*snipped chives*
*salt and freshly ground black pepper*

Dry the potatoes well and bake in a hot oven until soft. Leave to cool, then cut each lengthwise into four. Scoop out the majority of the flesh (use in another dish), and then deep-fry skins, a few at a time, until brown and crisp. Drain very well and keep warm.

To make the dip, simply mix all the remaining ingredients together. Serve either on a communal platter with the bowl of cream in the centre, or on individual plates.

Serves 4

# STOVIES

Potatoes are important in Scottish cookery, and have been so since the mid-18th century when they became a Scottish field crop. At its simplest, stovies combines potatoes and onions, but it has many variations, some of which include fish, chicken or even limpets. Traditionally eaten on a Monday, this dish uses up the meat left over from the weekend roast. Stovies are cooked on top of the stove in a covered pan, the name deriving from the French *étouffé*, cooked in a closed vessel.

*2 lb (900g) floury potatoes, peeled*
*1 large onion, peeled*
*2 dessertspoons meat dripping*
*salt and freshly ground black pepper*
*leftover roast meat, cut into chunks*

Slice the potatoes thickly and the onion thinly. Soften the onion in the dripping in a large saucepan and then add potato slices, salt, pepper, meat and enough water to come, at most, ½ in (1.25cm) up the sides of the pan.

Cover the pan tightly and cook gently, shaking every now again, until potatoes are tender (at least 30 minutes). Don't uncover the pan until you are sure they are ready.

Serves 4

# IRISH STEW

This Irish basic is very similar to the hotpot of Lancashire, where potatoes were first cultivated in England. The stew could be baked in the oven, at 350°F/180°C/Gas 4 for 2–2½ hours.

*2½ lb (1.1kg) mutton or lamb chops or cutlets, not too thin*
*salt and freshly ground black pepper*
*1 lb (450g) onions, peeled and thickly sliced*
*8 oz (225g) carrots, trimmed and thickly sliced (optional)*
*1½ lb (675g) potatoes, peeled and thickly sliced*
*water or stock*

Cut surplus fat from meat and melt in a frying pan. Quickly brown the meat, then lay half in the bottom of a large, tall flameproof casserole. Season well, then cover with a layer of onion and carrot slices (if using), followed by a layer of potato slices. Repeat these layers and seasoning, ending with a layer of potatoes arranged attractively over the top.

Pour in enough water (or stock) to half fill the casserole, cover tightly, and simmer for 2–2½ hours or until the meat is tender. Brown the top layer of potatoes if necessary under a hot grill or in a hot oven.

Serves 4

# LATKES

These potato pancakes are one of the great traditional Jewish dishes. Serve as a vegetable accompaniment or, without the onion and sprinkled with sugar and cinnamon, as a dessert.

*4 medium potatoes, peeled*
*1 medium onion, peeled*
*1 egg*
*salt and freshly ground black pepper*
*1/2 teaspoon bicarbonate of soda*
*butter, for frying*

Soak the potatoes for about 2 hours in cold water, then drain. Grate finely into a teatowel and press until quite dry. Place in a bowl, grate in the onion, then add the egg, some seasoning, and the bicarbonate. Mix well.

Heat the butter in a heavy frying pan and drop in dessertspoonfuls of the mixture. Cook gently until brown, then turn over and fry the other side. Drain well.

Serves 2–4

# GNOCCHI DI PATATE

Serve as a starter with a *pesto* sauce, or with melted butter and grated Parmesan, or with a good home-made tomato or meat sauce for a more substantial dish.

*1 lb (450g) potatoes, peeled, cut into 1in (2.5cm) cubes*
*salt and freshly ground black pepper*
*freshly grated nutmeg*
*4 tablespoons plain flour*
*1 small egg, beaten*
*butter*
*2 oz (50g) Parmesan cheese, grated*

Boil the potato cubes until tender, about 15 minutes. Drain and return to pan over heat to dry out. Rub through a coarse sieve, then season with lots of salt, pepper and nutmeg. Cool a little, then add the flour and egg, the latter gradually. The mixture should not be too sticky.

When smooth, turn out on to a floured board and knead. Roll to a sausage shape and cut off about 24 small pieces. Shape pieces into balls or flat circles.

Bring a large saucepan of salted water to the boil, and drop in a few *gnocchi* at a time. Poach until they rise to the surface of the water. Lift out with a slotted spoon, drain well, and place in a well buttered serving dish. Pour about 2 oz (50g) melted butter over the *gnocchi* and sprinkle with grated cheese.

Serves 2–4

# RÖSTI

This Swiss potato cake, normally served with sausages, is good with grilled bacon and fried eggs on top.

A similar 'pan cake', from Northumberland, is Panhaggerty. Meaning simply 'onions and potatoes', it is layers of grated or sliced raw potatoes and fried onions and, occasionally, cheese. The American version is hash browns, when boiled potatoes are diced and sautéed in bacon fat.

*1 lb (450g) even sized potatoes, washed*
*1 large onion, peeled*
*salt and freshly ground black pepper*
*2 oz (50g) butter*

Par-boil the potatoes for 7 minutes. Drain and leave to cool. Scrape the skins off and grate the potatoes and onion coarsely into a bowl. Season and mix well.

Using two frying pans, melt a quarter of the butter in each. Add half the potato mixture to each pan and stir around for about 5 minutes so that the shreds are butter coated and start to cook. Form the potato mixture in each pan into two round cakes, pressing down well. Fry for about 10 minutes and then remove from the pans, using two spatulas. Melt the remaining butter in the two pans, invert the cakes, and fry for a further 7–10 minutes to brown the other sides. Serve immediately.

Serves 4

# BUBBLE AND SQUEAK

This 19th-century dish of vegetable leftovers was named for the noise the ingredients make whilst frying. It is very similar in basic concept to the Irish dish Champ (mashed potatoes mixed with milk-poached leeks) and the same as another Irish dish, Colcannon. The amazingly named Rumblede-thumps from the Scottish borders is a mixture of mashed potatoes and cabbage, seasoned with cheese and chives.

*2 lb (900g) potatoes, cooked and peeled*
*2 oz (50g) butter*
*salt and freshly ground black pepper*
*1 medium cabbage (or Brussels sprouts), cooked and shredded*
*2 tablespoons plain flour*
*bacon fat, for frying*

Mash the potatoes with the butter and lots of salt and pepper, then mix with the cabbage.

Shape tablespoons of the mixture into round cakes, dust with flour, and fry in hot bacon fat until golden brown and crisp on both sides. Drain well before serving.

Serve 4–6

# GRATIN DAUPHINOIS

This is one of the most famous of the French potato gratin dishes, which consist of potato slices layered with ingredients such as butter, seasoning, cheese, chopped onion and garlic, moistened with stock, milk or cream, and baked until tender. A similar dish from Sweden, Jansson's Temptation, layers anchovy fillets and their oil with the potatoes. The American version, known as scalloped potatoes, adds onions and, occasionally, cheese.

*1 lb (450g) good firm potatoes, peeled*
*2 oz (50g) butter*
*salt and freshly ground black pepper*
*2 small garlic cloves, peeled and finely chopped*
*1/4 pint (150ml) double cream*
*1 teaspoon plain flour*
*1/4 pint (150ml) milk*
*freshly grated nutmeg*

Slice the potatoes very thinly, rinse to get rid of some of the starch, and dry thoroughly. Use some of the butter to grease a shallow gratin dish, then arrange a layer of potato slices in the bottom. Season well, and sprinkle on some of the chopped garlic. Cover with another layer of potatoes, seasonings and garlic, and continue until the potatoes are used up.

Mix the cream with the flour, then add the milk. Pour this over the potatoes and sprinkle the top with some nutmeg. Dot the remaining butter over the top and bake on the top shelf of the oven at 325°F/160°C/Gas 3 for 1–1¼ hours. Turn the heat up towards the end of cooking to brown the top if necessary.

Serves 2–4

# INDIAN POTATOES WITH SPINACH (SAAG ALOO)

Potatoes reached India in the late-18th century and were incorporated enthusiastically into the mainly vegetarian regional cuisines. Madhur Jaffrey's books, from one of which this recipe is taken, are full of deliciously and uniquely spiced potato dishes.

*2 lb (900g) waxy potatoes, peeled and cut into ¾ in (2cm) cubes*
*salt*
*1 lb (450g) fresh spinach*
*6 tablespoons vegetable oil*
*½ teaspoon whole mustard seeds*
*1 large onion, peeled and chopped*
*2 cloves garlic, peeled and finely chopped*
*1 teaspoon garam masala*
*a tiny pinch of cayenne pepper (optional)*

Put the potato dice into boiling water with 1 table-spoon salt, and bring back to the boil. Cover, reduce heat, and cook for about 6 minutes. Drain, spread potato out, and leave to cool.

Wash spinach carefully and drop into a large pan of boiling water to wilt. Drain and squeeze as dry as possible, then chop.

Heat oil in a large non-stick frying pan over a medium to high heat. When very hot, put in mustard seeds and as soon as they start to pop (within a few seconds), add onion and garlic. Turn heat down to medium and fry for 3–4 minutes until onion is lightly brown. Add the chopped spinach and stir-fry for another 10 minutes. Add the potato dice, 1 teaspoon salt, the *garam masala* and cayenne if using. Stir and mix gently until potatoes are heated through.

Serves 6

**Note:** If a casserole is over salty or over spiced, a few slices of peeled potato cooked in it will absorb the salt or the heat.

# POTATO AND CELERIAC PURÉE

A classic French potato purée (or mashed potato) can be made as below, by simply omitting the celeriac and doubling the potato quantity to serve four.

Aligot, another traditional French dish, mixes a little more double cream (or *crème fraîche*) and 12 oz (350g) grated Cantal or Gruyère cheese into the basic 2 lb (900g) potato purée. The cheese is beaten into the purée over heat, when it forms ribbons which have to be cut (*aligoté*) for serving.

*1 lb (450g) floury potatoes, boiled and peeled*
*2 oz (50g) butter*
*3 tablespoons double cream, heated*
*salt and freshly ground black pepper*
*1 lb (450g) celeriac, scrubbed*

While the potatoes are still hot, reduce to a purée with a masher or by pushing through a sieve. Add the butter, hot cream and seasonings and mix thoroughly.

Meanwhile, quickly peel the celeriac, then cut into ¼ in (6mm) cubes. Work fast as celeriac discolours. Boil in salted water for about 6 minutes until soft, then drain well. Dry out over a low heat, then purée as above.

Blend the celeriac purée with the potato purée, and taste for seasoning. Heat through gently before serving.

Serves 4

# NEW POTATOES WITH SAVOURY BUTTER

Tiny new potatoes are delicious when simply boiled with a sprig of mint, and topped with butter.

*2 lb (900g) small, even-sized new potatoes*
*salt*
*a generous handful of fresh mint*
*2 oz (50g) butter*
*1 small garlic clove, peeled and crushed*
*1½ tablespoons each freshly chopped parsley and chives*

Wash the potatoes, but don't scrub them if you can help it. Put them in a pan, with any larger ones to the bottom. Pour in enough boiling water to come about half-way up the potatoes, then add some salt and a sprig of the mint. Cover tightly and cook for about 20 minutes or until just tender.

Melt the butter gently, cook the garlic for a minute or two, then mix in the parsley, chives and the remaining mint, chopped. Drain the potatoes well, and pour the savoury butter over them, agitating the pan so that each potato is coated.

Serves 4–6

The colloquial phrase 'small potatoes' (US) means something or someone is not worth much. If something is 'the potato', it, he or she is the real thing, correct or excellent.

# POTATO SALAD

Lighten a 'mayonnaise' for potato salad by using half yoghurt. You could also mix in some finely chopped spring onions or mild Spanish onion for additional flavour.

*1 lb (450g) new or waxy maincrop potatoes, washed*
*French dressing*
*¼ pint (150ml) good mayonnaise*
*5 oz (150g) natural yoghurt*
*snipped chives*
*salt and freshly ground black pepper*
*paprika*

Boil the potatoes in their skins in salted water, drain, cool slightly, then peel. Leave small new potatoes whole, slice maincrop. Toss them while still hot in enough French dressing to coat, then leave to cool completely and absorb the dressing.

Mix the mayonnaise, yoghurt and the majority of the chives and season with salt and pepper. Spoon over the potatoes and sprinkle with remaining chives and a little paprika.

Serves 4

# POTATO SCONES

These thin triangular-shaped scones are a Scottish and Irish speciality, but are also known in Lancashire. Serve freshly made for tea with butter, jam or honey, flat or rolled up. Alternatively, fry them and serve with grilled bacon etc. for breakfast.

*1½ lb (675g) floury potatoes, peeled and boiled*
*salt*
*6 oz (175g) plain flour*

Sieve potatoes on to a floured board and add salt to taste. Gradually mix in the flour, kneading it lightly.

Roll mixture out as thinly as possible and cut into large rounds the size of a dinner plate. Cut each round into farls (or quarters), prick well and bake on a hot griddle or girdle for 7–10 minutes, turning once.

Makes about 16

# POTATO BREADROLLS

This recipe comes from a British Potato Marketing Board leaflet. The same dough can be used for croissants, for a pizza base, and for a 2 lb (900g) loaf. For the loaf, put the knocked back dough into a greased tin, brush with milk, prove for 45 minutes and bake at the same temperature as below for 50 minutes.

*2 teaspoons dried yeast*
*a pinch of sugar*
*½ pint (300ml) warm water*
*1 lb (450g) strong white flour*
*2 teaspoons salt*
*4 oz (125g) good potatoes, peeled, cooked and sieved*

TOPPING
*milk or beaten egg, to glaze*
*sesame or poppy seeds (optional)*

Sprinkle the yeast and sugar into the warm water, stir and leave for about 10 minutes until frothy. Sift the flour and salt into a bowl and rub in the sieved potato. Stir the yeast liquid into the flour and mix to form a dough.

Turn the dough on to a floured surface and knead until smooth, elastic and no longer sticky (about 10 minutes). Place it in an oiled polythene bag and leave in a warm place for about an hour, or until doubled in size.

Knock the dough back and knead for about a minute. Divide into 16 pieces. Shape into rolls, plaits, cottage loaves or knots, then brush with milk or beaten egg and sprinkle with seeds if liked. Cover and leave to prove for about 25 minutes.

Bake at 450°F/230°C/Gas 8 for 15 minutes, or until the rolls sound hollow when tapped on the bottom.

Makes 16

Mr. East gave a feast;
Mr. North laid the cloth;
Mr. West did his best;
Mr. South burnt his mouth
With eating a cold potato.

# POTATO FOLKLORE

* In ancient Peru, women fortune-tellers used potatoes for divination. They would pick up tubers in pairs from a heap, and if none was left at the end, the omens for the coming year were favourable.

* For the best crops, potatoes should be planted on Good Friday. Even when Easter falls as much as a month later than normal, planting is often postponed in order to synchronise with Good Friday – and then in Ireland the ridges are often sprinkled with holy water for good measure.

* If planted on Good Friday, first earlies should be lifted on Whit Monday, the seventh after Easter.

* In Galway, in the Republic of Ireland, the day on which the first digging of potatoes is permitted is Garland Sunday, the last in July; in Kerry, it's the 7th July, the local saint's day; in Cork, some potatoes must be dug on the 29th June.

* A peeled potato carried in a pocket on the same side as an aching tooth will, as it dries, cure the tooth.

* A pregnant woman should not eat potatoes, especially at night, if she wishes her child to have a small head.

# OTHER USES FOR POTATOES

## HEALTH AND MEDICINE

Folk medicine, and many present-day advocates of natural health, credit the potato with beneficial properties. A glass of raw potato juice helps cleanse the system, countering constipation. Potato juice or raw mashed potato used as a liniment is said to help many rheumatic complaints (a raw tuber carried in the pocket was believed to have the same effect), and to help haemorrhoids and chilblains.

A potato poultice – grated raw potato between two pieces of gauze – relieves minor sunburn. Similarly, the pain and heat of a minor burn can be alleviated by covering it with a slice of raw potato.

## BEAUTY

When applied directly to the face, potato juice is good for skin problems, even for eczema. A face mask for greasy or wrinkled skins can be made from potato juice and Fuller's Earth, or simply rub the face with raw potato. A cleansing hand cream can be concocted from some cooked potatoes mixed with a little glycerine, safflower oil and rosewater. To ease tired, puffy or 'baggy' eyes, simply cover with slices of raw potato.

# HOUSEHOLD

*Household Advice* (1855) claimed that chopped raw potatoes and warm water shaken together in an old decanter or bottle would clean the inaccessible inside. And *Success Magazine* (1870) advocated the cleaning of oil paintings by rubbing gently with a half raw potato; slice the top surface off as it becomes dirty.

Silver can be cleaned by plunging into the water in which potatoes have boiled. Minor burns in carpets can often be removed by rubbing with a raw potato: when the juice dries to a powder, brush off gently and repeat for best results.

The safest way of cleaning old and delicate embroidery is to cover with a layer of slightly warmed potato flour: before it cools completely, brush off with a very soft brush.

Half a raw potato can de-ice a frozen windscreen, and all artistic infants know about potato cuts – halved raw potatoes cut in relief, dipped in paint, and then pressed on to paper.

Dried potato peelings can help light fires; and a small piece of raw potato placed in tin, jar or pouch will keep tobacco from becoming too dry.

*To Clean an Old Silk Dress*
'Unpick the dress, and brush it with a velvet brush. Then grate two large potatoes into a quart of water; let it stand to settle; strain it off quite clear, and sponge the dress with it. Iron it on the wrong side, as the ironed side will be shiny.' From 'Useful Receipts for Housekeepers and Servants' in *Warne's Model Cookery and Housekeeping Book*, 1868.

## ACKNOWLEDGEMENTS

Thanks are due to the following: CMA, Bonn; Cyprus Trade Centre; Embassy of the Soviet Union; *Eurofruit*; Donald MacLean; Potato Marketing Board; J. Sainsbury plc; Waitrose Ltd; Walkers Crisps Ltd.

A vital source of every kind of information on the potato has been *The History and Social Influence of the Potato* by R. Salaman (Cambridge University Press, 1949). Also fascinating were *Seeds of Change* by H. Hobhouse (Sidgwick and Jackson, 1985), *Food* by W. Root (Simon & Schuster, 1980), and *On Food and Cooking* by H. McGee (Allen & Unwin, 1986).

# OTHER TITLES IN THE SERIES

The Little Green Avocado Book
The Little Garlic Book
The Little Pepper Book
The Little Lemon Book
The Little Apple Book
The Little Strawberry Book
The Little Mustard Book
The Little Honey Book
The Little Nut Book
The Little Mushroom Book
The Little Bean Book
The Little Rice Book
The Little Tea Book
The Little Coffee Book
The Little Chocolate Book
The Little Curry Book
The Little Mediterranean Food Book
The Little Exotic Vegetable Book
The Little Exotic Fruit Book
The Little Yoghurt Book
The Little Tofu Book
The Little Breakfast Book
The Little Egg Book